YOUR KNOWLEDGE HAS VALUE

- We will publish your bachelor's and master's thesis, essays and papers

- Your own eBook and book - sold worldwide in all relevant shops

- Earn money with each sale

Upload your text at www.GRIN.com and publish for free

Bibliographic information published by the German National Library:

The German National Library lists this publication in the National Bibliography; detailed bibliographic data are available on the Internet at http://dnb.dnb.de .

This book is copyright material and must not be copied, reproduced, transferred, distributed, leased, licensed or publicly performed or used in any way except as specifically permitted in writing by the publishers, as allowed under the terms and conditions under which it was purchased or as strictly permitted by applicable copyright law. Any unauthorized distribution or use of this text may be a direct infringement of the author s and publisher s rights and those responsible may be liable in law accordingly.

Imprint:

Copyright © 2017 GRIN Verlag
Print and binding: Books on Demand GmbH, Norderstedt Germany
ISBN: 9783668655218

This book at GRIN:

https://www.grin.com/document/414677

Sylvia Ruvimbo Matsika

Sovereignty over Natural Resources

GRIN Verlag

GRIN - Your knowledge has value

Since its foundation in 1998, GRIN has specialized in publishing academic texts by students, college teachers and other academics as e-book and printed book. The website www.grin.com is an ideal platform for presenting term papers, final papers, scientific essays, dissertations and specialist books.

Visit us on the internet:

http://www.grin.com/

http://www.facebook.com/grincom

http://www.twitter.com/grin_com

Table of Contents

SOVEREIGNTY OVER NATURAL WEALTH AND RESOURCES 2

    Sovereignty over Natural Resources as a Principle of International Law 2

    Principle Subjects and Right Holders and Objects of Resource Sovereignty 3

    Declaration on Permanent Sovereignty over Natural Resources 3

    The United Nations Declaration on the Rights of Indigenous Peoples 5

    Legal Status of Permanent Sovereignty over Natural Resources 5

    Zimbabwe Case Study 7

    Conclusion 8

    Bibliography 9

SOVEREIGNTY OVER NATURAL WEALTH AND RESOURCES

The ability of States to be independent and have autonomy and supreme control over their internal affairs subject to limitations of public international law is known as state sovereignty. All States have exclusive jurisdiction to administer and control matters within their borders. The territory of a State is not only limited to the land but includes, airspace, territorial sea, exclusive economic zones and the continental shelf for coastal States. No state or international organ may interfere in issues that are within the jurisdiction of another state. State sovereignty encompasses a lot of dimensions within a country, one of them being sovereignty over natural resources. Sovereignty over natural resources is a complex and powerful organising principle in world politics which emerged in the post-1945 period and has been affirmed in various international legal instruments. Due to its complexity, the permanent sovereignty principle has not however risen to jus cogens status in international law.

Sovereignty over Natural Resources as a Principle of International Law

The genesis of permanent sovereignty has its roots in the power struggles of Latin America and Africa. In Latin America, the newly independent States viewed permanent sovereignty as a tool of economic and political independence. In Africa, it was meant to aid the decolonisation process and bring about the self-determination of the peoples. Political self-determination could only be achieved through economic determination and sovereignty over natural resources was a key component to bring about economic sovereignty and development by restricting further exploitation by colonial powers and strengthen political standing.

The highly controversial matter was brought before the United Nations General Assembly as a means of acquiring an internationally enforced legal shield against claims of property and contractual rights claims and by former colonial powers. Resolution 1803 (XVII) provided protection to under-developed States from exploitation by other States and international organisations by enforcing that the sovereignty of the peoples and States over their natural wealth and resources be strictly respected. Initially, these rights were privy to decolonised States, developing States and undeveloped States but expanded to include all States in the 1970's.

The General Assembly adopted resolution 1803 (XVII) on the "Permanent Sovereignty over Natural Resources" in 1962. The principle of sovereignty over natural resources gives States the right to freely dispose natural resources within their jurisdiction including marine resources subject to the United Nations Convention on the Law of the Sea (UNCLOS) and other legal instruments. The scope of resource sovereignty broadened over the years to include the right to self-determination of natural resources by indigenous peoples and also to include the rights and related duties of States and peoples that are derived from the principle.

Principle Subjects and Right Holders and Objects of Resource Sovereignty

Sovereignty over natural resources unlike other principles of state sovereignty is not only privy to the State but has other principle subjects and rights holders. The primary right holders of sovereignty are the peoples but more often this right is suppressed by the State. It has been argued that the whole of humankind are right holders not only those in the territory in question. Peoples in occupied territories are also considered as subjects and right holders, for example, the people of Palestine as reflected in the Israeli War Opinion. The United Nations Declaration on the Rights of Indigenous Peoples (UNDRIP) which was adopted by the General Assembly in September 2007, extended the right to self-determination to indigenous peoples and this resulted in indigenous peoples having sovereignty over natural resources within their territories although it is subject to limitations by the State. In 1974, Christopher Stone published a book entitled *"Should trees have standing?"* in which he explored the idea that natural objects should have rights, however that concept has not materialised in international law but could possibly be explored in the future.

Objects of this principle include living, non-living, exhaustible and non-exhaustible natural resources. Natural wealth which is the base of the natural resources is also an object of resource sovereignty. Other objects include national and cultural resources, environmental utilisation space and vital ecological functions.

Declaration on Permanent Sovereignty over Natural Resources

The Declaration on Permanent Sovereignty over Natural Resources set out eight principles relating to the disposition and exploration of natural resources, foreign investment and other issues concerning the matter. The rights conferred upon right holders of sovereignty over natural resources has corresponding duties which will be discussed below.

The Declaration attributes the right to permanent sovereignty to peoples and States in the interest of national development. The subjects of the Declaration have the right to;

a) possess, dispose of, explore, exploit, develop and market their natural resources
b) manage, preserve and conserve the natural resources
c) regulate foreign capital investment; and
d) Nationalise, expropriate foreign property subject to international law requirements.

The rights derived from the Declaration have become blurred to the unstable notion of state sovereignty in this century. Strife's, wars, political woes and struggles have resulted in state sovereignty being abandoned, which has left the resources subject to abuse and exploitation by other people and States. Often at times, international law is a tool that is used to override the sovereignty of a nation and sometimes international law can be used a tool of exploitation by more powerful states to quash sovereignty of weaker nations so as to get access to their resources although this is subject to debate and interpretation. Sovereignty is subject to interpretation and therefore the fate of sovereignty over natural resources is left hanging in the balance.

The resource related duties are but not limited to;

a) use resources for national development and well-being of the people of the nation
b) sustainable exploration, disposition and due care to the environment
c) prudent resource management and fulfilment of resource rights in good faith
d) observe international law, world economic duties and world environment duties
e) respect other right holders
f) Cooperation and knowledge sharing for worldwide sustainable development.

The rights and duties that arise from permanent sovereignty have to be examined and balanced. States and other subjects of permanent resource sovereignty often neglect the duties associated with the rights as they only seek to assert the rights without any care of the duties. None of the subjects of permanent sovereignty can derogate from the rule of law which does not immunise them from the responsibilities and duties that correspond to the rights. Although States have jurisdiction over their internal matters, they are not above the domestic or international law.

The United Nations Declaration on the Rights of Indigenous Peoples

The United Nations Declaration on the Rights of Indigenous Peoples was adopted by the General Assembly in 2007. It addresses the indigenous peoples right to self-determination, non-discrimination, life and integrity, cultural identity and heritage, an educational system and health services, as well as the rights to their lands and resources[1]. The Declaration asserts the rights of indigenous peoples to their land and resources within their territory. The Declaration, however, does not vest permanent sovereignty over natural resources within their territories. The indigenous people, however, have rights to be consulted and engaged by governments in the decision making concerning their natural resource management by the State

Territories of indigenous people should be respected as they have rights to their habitats and to State protection. Indigenous peoples rights are sometimes ignored and trampled on the by the State so as to advance other interests of the State. The controversial Dakota Access Pipeline case, where the Standing Rock Indian Reservation in North Dakota, lost the battle to stop the Dakota Access Pipeline from being buried under their sacred waters of Lake Oahe, is an example of how States fail to observe the rights of indigenous people and respect and protect their habitats. The lack of exclusive and permanent sovereignty of natural resources of the indigenous peoples will always leave them vulnerable to the abuse of their rights to their ancestral lands.

Legal Status of Permanent Sovereignty over Natural Resources

Although United Nations declarations tend to be mere recommendations without a legal binding force, some resolutions do however surpass this status without much controversy. Permanent Sovereignty over Natural Resources emerged as soft law but was later on evolved and was incorporated in treaty law. It is referred to in judicial decisions by human rights courts and tribunals. Permanent sovereignty is recognised in doctrine and was viewed as a customary principle of international law by the International Court of Justice in 2005. Nicolaas Schrijver, argues that permanent sovereignty has not risen to the status of "jus cogens", a principle in international law that cannot be derogated from because a state sovereignty can be revoked

---

[1] Self-determination of peoples and sovereignty over natural wealth and resources Nicolaas Schrijver*

subject to international law. Permanent sovereignty over natural resources does not have the power to dethrone other principles of international law.

The incorporation of permanent sovereignty into treaty law is reflected in various international instruments. International commodity agreements give power or sovereignty to the commodity exporting countries over their natural resources. The United Nations Convention on the Law of the Sea is another international treaty that awards coastal States permanent sovereignty over their natural resources. These treaties also lay out obligations that States have in conjunction with the rights. Various human rights treaties and conventions on armed conflict also confer the rights and duties of permanent sovereignty over natural resources. An example of such incorporation is emulated in the Protocol Against the Illegal Exploitation of Natural Resources which was adopted in November 2006. Article 3(1) states that;

"Member States shall freely dispose of their natural resources. This right shall be exercised in the exclusive interest of the people. In no case, the populations shall a State be deprived of it"[2]

In the case of Congo v. Uganda (2005), the International Court of Justice examined whether there was any to illegal exploitation of Congolese natural resources by Uganda. The principles of permanent sovereignty over natural resources were discussed. The Democratic Republic of Congo argued that Uganda had failed to respect its sovereignty over its territory, natural resources and the peoples rights to self-determination by engaging in military and paramilitary activities and by the illegal violation and plundering of Congolese natural resources. General Assembly resolution 1803 (XVII) on Permanent Sovereignty over Natural Resources was referred during the trial. Uganda denied that it had the principle of permanent sovereignty over natural resources on the basis that the principle was set as part of the decolonisation process and did not apply to the case at hand and that the looting had been carried by military personnel in their personal capacity. The Court held that the principle of Congo's sovereignty over its natural resources had not been violated. The Court concluded that the principle of permanent sovereignty over natural resources is an important of this principle of customary international law but it did not apply in this situation because the exploitation of Congo's natural resources was by intervening members of Uganda's military.

---

[2] Protocol Against the Illegal Exploitation of Natural Resources November 2006

Zimbabwe Case Study

General Assembly Resolution 523(VI) asserted the rights of developing and under developed nations to freely dispose of their natural resources for economic development and for the well-being of the people incongruity with the State's national interests. Exploitation and disposition of natural resources can create revenue to aid States in sustainable development. Even after the decolonisation process, some former colonies, especially in Africa, still struggle with the issue of sovereignty as they are constant efforts to undermine their sovereignty and permanent sovereignty over natural resources by more powerful States.

Zimbabwe, a former British colony gained independence in April 1980. The people of Zimbabwe, after having been deprived by the colonial power to the right to be subjects of permanent sovereignty over natural resources believed that independence would bring about much-needed change. The government that has been in power since 1980, has failed time and time again to dispose of the natural resources for national development and the well-being of the people. Zimbabwean government just like many African governments has abused their sovereignty over natural resources by quashing the rights of the peoples to the resources and by completely ignoring their obligations and duties emanating from the right to sovereignty over natural resources that stem from domestic and international law. The rule of law is often abandoned in Zimbabwe by the State so as to advance their personal agendas neglecting their duties to the people of the nation.

The case of Zimbabwe illustrates how the duties arising from permanent sovereignty over natural resources even though recognised in international treaty law are set aside. Zimbabwe is rich in a number of natural resources including, gold, platinum, nickel and most recently diamonds. The government could apply the principle of permanent sovereignty over its diamonds as a tool to foster development. The African Charter on Human and Peoples' Rights states in Article 1, that permanent sovereignty shall be exercised in the exclusive interest of the people. Sovereignty although exercised fails to promote national development. The Constitution of Zimbabwe is the supreme law of the land and any law, practice, custom or conduct inconsistent with it is invalid to the extent of the inconsistency[3]. Zimbabwe follows a monist approach with regards to customary international law and a dualist approach to international treaty law to the extent of its consistency with laws of Zimbabwe. International

---

[3] S1 of Constitution of Zimbabwe Amendment (No. 20) Act, 2013.

treaties that Zimbabwe has ratified are only binding to the country when they are incorporated into domestic law.

The domestic mining laws confer the custodial right over the country's mineral resources in the President. The vesting of rights over natural resources in the President created an opportunity for abuse and limits the rights of other beneficiaries under international law. The lack of good governance in the management of the natural resources has resulted in the blurred transparency of how revenue from the diamond sales is utilised. Zimbabwe has a long history of abandoning its international obligations in international human rights law and other areas and it has often been slapped with economic sanctions that have further crippled the economy and the abuse of permanent sovereignty over resources is no different.

Conclusion

The issue of permanent sovereignty over natural resources is still an ongoing debate and the principle is likely to be developed further into new political and legal principles and concepts. In future generations to come, the concept of state sovereignty may be completely eroded by the exponential growth of private capitalism. There has been a growing trend in international economics that has resulted in economic activities undermining the sovereignty of States. International trade and economics have encouraged a change in approach to the exploitation of natural resources moving towards functional regimes and forgoing territorial regimes. A lot of environmental policies are being developed to ensure more sustainable developed and prevent further derogatory harm to the environment and these policies affect and limit State's permanent sovereignty over natural resources.

Changes in State's public policies towards more democratic States had resulted in more public participation in decision making. This awards all the subjects holders the rights to the natural resources without the State trampling on those rights but still retaining control over the management of the resources. Indigenous peoples rights are getting more and more attention and their territorial rights could one day evolve into permanent sovereignty. The principle of permanent sovereignty continues to take new directions. There have been developments in international humanitarian law of how to address rights and duties of subjects in occupied territories. The Declaration on permanent sovereignty is still an important and dynamic international legal instrument.

Bibliography

1) Asiimwe, P. (2004). Report of the UN Panel of Experts on the Illegal Exploitation of Natural Resources of the Democratic Republic of the Congo. Journal of Energy & Natural Resources Law, 22(2), pp.194-200.
2) Constitution of Zimbabwe Amendment (No. 20) Act, 2013.
3) Human Rights Law in Africa, E. (2004). Protocol To The African Charter On Human And Peoples' Rights On The Establishment Of An African Court On Human And Peoples' Rights. Human Rights Law in Africa Online, 1(1), pp.170-174.
4) Okowa, P. (2006). II. Case Concerning Armed Activities on the Territory of the Congo (The Democratic Republic of the Congo v Uganda). International and Comparative Law Quarterly, 55(03), pp.742-753.
5) Permanent Sovereignty Over Natural Resources. Resolution Adopted by the United Nations General Assembly at Its 1194th Plenary Meeting, December 14, 1962. (1963). The American Journal of International Law, 57(3), p.710.
6) Simmonds, T. (2007). A Dictionary of Law (6th edition) 2007 Edited by Elizabeth A. Martin and Jonathan Law. A Dictionary of Law (6th edition). Oxford: Oxford University Press 2006. vii +590 pp., ISBN: 978 0 19 280698 7 £11.99. Reference Reviews, 21(2), pp.026-27.
7) Stoett, P. and Schrijver, N. (1998). Sovereignty over Natural Resources: Balancing Rights and Duties. International Journal, 53(3), p.599.
8) United Nations Declaration on the Rights of Indigenous Peoples. (2007). International Journal of Cultural Property, 14(04).

YOUR KNOWLEDGE HAS VALUE

- We will publish your bachelor's and master's thesis, essays and papers

- Your own eBook and book - sold worldwide in all relevant shops

- Earn money with each sale

Upload your text at www.GRIN.com and publish for free